WALK[illegible]
COMPASS

living a life directed by the holy spirit

CASEY **HODGES**

ˈedə,fī
EDIFI PUBLISHING

Compass
Living a life directed by the Holy Spirit

Published by Edifi Publishing
3446 Winder Highway
Suite M195
Flowery Branch, GA 30542

info@edifipublishing.com
www.edifipublishing.com

Edited by Hannah Price and Ruth Woodson
Cover design & layout by Gloria Stella
Author photo by Taty Streetman

ISBN: 978-1-7339305-8-1

Printed and bound in the United States of America

10 9 8 7 6 5 4 3 2 1

To all those who have taught me to
rely on the compass of the Holy Spirit
and to yield to its direction.

CONTENTS

ACKNOWLEDGEMENTS

First, I would like to give praise to God for entrusting me with this revelation and the ability to take each step to get this book published.

I would like to thank my lovely wife who supported me and pushed me to finish when I felt stuck in doing something as new as writing this book.

Thank you to all those who supported and cheered me on while I was writing.

To Pastor Robert and Gloria Stella for believing in me and helping me publish this dream of mine.

To Hannah Price and Ruth Woodson for editing.

For those who will read and share this book with family, friends and your circle of influence - thank you!

INTRODUCTION

Thank you for picking up this book and giving it a chance. I wrote this book with the desire to help people receive a clear understanding of how to effectively navigate through life. No matter the season you find yourself in, you did not end up here by accident. If you are reading these words, it's safe to say you are alive and breathing - which means you are also trying your best to navigate this life. Don't worry, we all are, but how do we do that?

My prayer for this book is to help you to understand God's directional plans for your life. As you begin reading, I challenge you to remove any distractions that may hinder you from listening to the leading of the Holy Spirit. Allow yourself some time for reflection, to develop a new perspective, and really lean into what God may be speaking to you.

CHAPTER 1

THE COMPASS

The heart of man plans his way,

but the Lord establishes his steps.

Proverbs 16:9 ESV

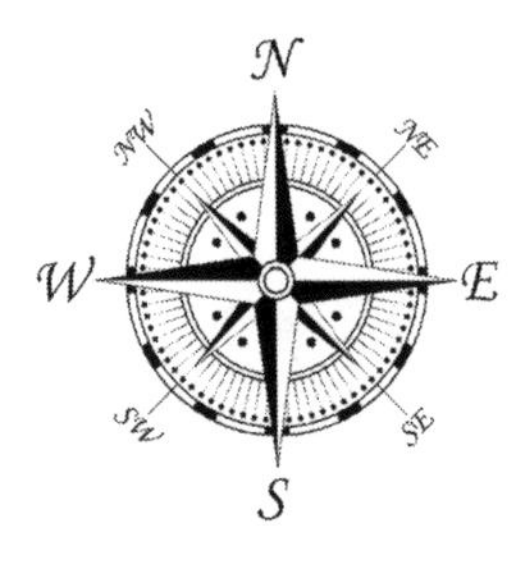

CHAPTER 1

THE COMPASS

My inspiration for writing this book was a simple tool called a compass. A compass is small but can have a great impact on a journey and destination. Before the invention of the compass, early explorers navigated with only the sun and stars as their guide. This led to frequent shipwrecks and lost travelers during stormy or cloudy weather.

A compass shows you the relative direction of one of four cardinal directions by using the earth's magnetic field. It is one of the greatest inventions from ancient times. The compass is an ideal tool for any traveler or explorer and is still used today to navigate the natural world around us and help lost people along their journey. When was the last time you used a compass? Believe it or not you do more than you think.

Since the creation of mobile GPS, many of us are not used to using a compass or directional terms as early travelers did. It seems in modern times that a sense of real direction is unheard of in our daily lives. You would probably be surprised if I gave you a compass and expected you to find your way through the Amazon Forest or even the concrete jungle of New York. I'm pretty sure a man hunt would have to take place to come and rescue you.

When I moved from my hometown to where my wife and I currently live, I had to navigate using mobile apps because I was unfamiliar with my surroundings. I even had to use my phone to get to the church where I currently work. I can't even begin to think of the time it would take if I had only a paper road map to get me to an unfamiliar destination, much less a compass. Most of us have never actually used a compass except to maybe pick one up as a kid and go around in circles.

However, early travelers depended on these tools when sailing across the sea. Can you imagine if they would have had Google Maps on their ships hundreds of years ago? It probably would have said things like, "save 5 minutes by going left at the next wave" or "whale crossing ahead, expect traffic." (It's ok to laugh at my cheesy jokes). Even just a few decades ago, before GPS was integrated into our cars and phones, people would have to stop at gas stations and go in to ask for directions (just like any country song explains). Nowadays, that's something you would only see in the movies or if you are some cool millennial hippy with a flip phone.

A Compass for Our Life

I think we can all agree that directions are a key part of our everyday lives, but when was the last time you looked to see if you were going north or west or even northeast or southwest? Do me a favor the next time you are out driving or walking around and check which direction you are going. Today, we have the tools to make traveling easier. We depend heavily on our phones and GPS to tell us where we need to go, but what about the calling and direction for our lives? Google Maps cannot help with that.

Every day of our lives is a new experience and everyone's journey in life is different. But at some point, we all ask similar questions, "God, where do I go from here?" or "What is your direction for my life?" These are questions that modern navigational tools cannot help answer. Without direction, we can begin to feel confused, frustrated and lost.

When my wife and I travel together somewhere new, she is usually the one with the directions pulled up on her phone. As we travel, she typically begins to look up something else instead of focusing on the navigation. I quickly begin to lose my sense of direction, constantly having to ask, "Where do I go?" because I don't have the help that I need.

Thankfully, God has provided us with a simple navigational tool to help guide us through answering these questions. He has given us a compass for our lives. This compass helps to keep us on the right path in order to reach His desired destination for us and helps us to navigate difficulties, hardships, and even great successes.

Almost everything we do, begins as a desire from within our hearts: from the car that we drive, to the food that we eat and even how we fix our hair. We like what we see and we try to obtain what we want. Over time, the ways of a man's heart will create the state of the man. Christ gives us the freedom to plan the direction of our lives from day to day, making decisions as to how we are led. But one thing remains true for those who may desire it: though we may make plans for our life's direction, "the LORD establishes our steps." My heart will lead me in my desires, but God within my heart will lead me into His promise - life's abundance.

The Compass of the Holy Spirit

How can you know the difference between where your desires are leading you and what God is doing within your heart to lead you in His ways? The simple answer is as scripture tells us "to walk in the spirit and we will not carry out the things of the flesh" (Gal. 5:16, my paraphrase). This can be accomplished by simply being sensitive towards the Holy Spirit; yielding to His voice and being obedient to it. As we learn this, we will begin to see the work of the Holy Spirit in our lives as the "compass" which leads us.

My heart will lead me
in my desires, but God
within my heart will lead
me into His promise -
life's abundance.

@caseyhodges
#walkingwithacompass

One thing to know before we move on is this assurance. Christ gave us help. He poured out His spirit for us to use as a tool and helper in our lives, to lead us and guide us. That has been the faith within my heart - to know that even if I desire to go one way, through the leading of the Holy Spirit and by obedience to God, He will establish my steps and lead me into the right direction.

The compass of the Holy Spirit is the greatest tool ever given to us. It packs a mighty punch in being effective, but only if we become sensitive to its leading. If you have never received the Holy Spirit personally, I encourage you to take time before you continue reading and ask God to impart His Spirit in you. Receive it and believe it is so. Trust me, as the famous minister Larry Lee said it "get on your knees and pray. You will know when you have received it." (my paraphrase)

"And Peter said to them, "Repent and be baptized every one of you in the name of Jesus Christ for the forgiveness of your sins, and you will receive the gift of the Holy Spirit."
Acts 2:38 ESV

The compass of the Holy Spirit is the greatest tool ever given to us. It packs a mighty punch in being effective, but only if we become sensitive to its leading.

@caseyhodges
#walkingwithacompass

CHAPTER 2

SAY "YES"

Do not despise these small beginnings, for the Lord rejoices to see the work begin...

Zechariah 4:10 NLT

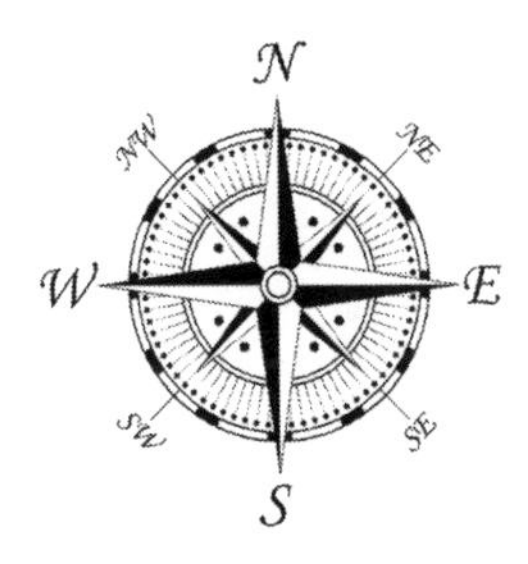

CHAPTER 2

SAY "YES"

Moses was born to a Levite mother but raised by an Egyptian woman. Even though he was raised differently, he still knew his identity. As he became older, he found himself going to see his people more and more. The oppression that was upon them made him so angry, he even killed a man.

Like us, Moses was not perfect. His sin of murder soon found him out, and he fled out of fear. However, this low moment in his life led him to one of the greatest moments recorded in the Bible: when at the burning bush, he found the call of God. Through the burning bush, Moses heard the voice of God and the compass of the Holy Spirit was given to him. God showed him the way and led him from that day on. Moses needed only to obey.

Answering the Call

I remember high school and how fast it flew by. In the blink of an eye, I was a senior. If you are a senior, you know!. As the last school year comes around, everyone wants to know what you are going to do next. I made up something that sounded important and ambitious; something that would make some money and get me by and I began to chase that "dream."

About a year after graduation though, something in me began to feel different. I could sense a force pulling me into a different direction. My problem at that moment was I had never asked God what He thought. I began to search deep within myself, and I asked God for guidance.

That same year, I attended a youth conference and served as a leader with my church (fresh out of high school probably isn't someone to pick as a youth leader). After the first few nights, I could feel something shift within me. Maybe it was the lack of sleep or too much pizza every night, but the feeling never went away. One night, I felt the Holy Spirit leading me in a way I had never felt before and my whole life changed. It was no longer about what I wanted to do, but rather what God had planned for my life.

I went from wandering aimlessly to receiving the compass (direction) for my life. This direction pulled me and was asking me to make the changes and sacrifices needed to follow. I said, "yes," not really knowing that decision would change my whole life completely.

Like Moses, it was my burning bush. It was something I never thought would happen. That "yes" has challenged me and stretched me more than I could imagine. I had to leave the comfort of my hometown, the people I knew, and even the life I had planned for myself. But these things were soon identified as shackles of comfort and they needed to be broken off in order for me to step out.

I was charting through unknown territory, as if I had said "yes" to an unknown question. I didn't know what I was going to be doing in the next season of my life. I didn't know it would cost me more than anything that I could even imagine. I was a deer in headlights, just trying to see the other side of the road. I felt so unqualified and so lost in this new calling of mine. Honestly, I still struggle with this, and there are days where it throws its best punches.

You may find yourself battling through the lie of being unworthy or not being qualified to do the task and call on your life. Just remember the most important thing, WHO has our lives in His hands and what has He given us in ours - and that is the compass.

"But ye are a chosen generation, a royal priesthood, a holy nation, a peculiar people; that ye should shew forth the praises of him who hath called you out of darkness into his marvelous light"
1 Peter 2:9 KJV

You are Called

I have learned that this compass in my life doesn't lead me by my qualities or giftings, but the Holy Spirit leads me according to the plans of God. You will begin to see that the direction can grow the giftings that the destination will benefit from. He orders our steps. That burning bush was for a reason. That God shift in your life is for a purpose that you may or may not have yet seen. Moses, like all of us, tried to explain why he was not fit for the job and why he couldn't do it. He made his plea to God, and God told him otherwise.

God said, "I will be with you. And this will be the sign to you that it is I who have sent you: when you have brought the people out of Egypt, you will worship God on this mountain."
Exodus 3:12 NIV

Let us say that over ourselves. God is with us and He has sent us. The Bible says that we are called by God for his workmanship (Eph. 2:10). You are called by God for His good works! Let that be encouraging. No matter what doubts or fears you have, the God of the universe has called you for such a time as this. God looks upon his people and sees their burdens, and He calls people like you and I to be the answer in the world on His behalf.

What if that thing you've been complaining about is meant to be solved by you or that nation that is struggling might be saved because of you? God loves us so much that He doesn't just invite us into a relationship with Him, but He sets us apart and uses us for His glory and purpose. The only thing hindering us is not following the compass God provided for us through the power and influence of the Holy Spirit.

Moments like these will happen throughout life and it is God that brings us to these moments because we had a burning bush appointment. YOU have a burning bush appointment and God is there waiting for you. He will reveal His purpose to you - for you to reveal His Glory and to advance His Kingdom. The call on your life is the solution God has for a lost and hurting world. All you have to do is say "yes".

Into the Unknown

When God called me to full-time ministry, I had no idea what I was doing or how I would take my first step in that direction. I mean, I hadn't even read the whole bible by that point! However, that moment I felt called to the ministry was an incredible feeling, but also a terrifying one. The incredible part was I finally felt I had purpose in my life, but the terrifying part was I didn't have much direction. I had no idea what I was going to do.

The call on your life is
the solution God has for
a lost and hurting world.
All you have to do is
say "yes".

@caseyhodges
#walkingwithacompass

At first I thought, growing up in a small town, all I was going to be was a small-town preacher that had to work a full-time job as well; because that was what I knew. While there is nothing wrong with that, I soon felt that God did not want me to settle for what I could only grasp with my own mind and understanding. He wanted me to seek His best and to step out into the deep. I had a limited perspective but God had unlimited possibilities.

Now that I had received God's direction, it was time to gather support. It's always important to find Godly support for any journey. Moses had Aaron, David had Jonathan, and Elijah had Elisha. I knew that gaining the support of my parents would be the support I needed to be confident in answering the call in this season of my life. I know for a lot of you, you may not have the support of your parents and that only emphasizes the importance of finding someone much wiser that can be a spiritual parent.

During that time, I knew one thing was important to do and that was to *confess*. I knew that the moment I confessed God's direction with my mouth, it became real and there was no turning back. No joke, I told my parents I had something to tell them, and it took me an hour to get the words out. I wasn't shy, but for the first time, I felt that I was called, anointed, and appointed for all that God had for me and now was the time to step out in faith.

Stepping Out in Faith

I remember when it was time for me to move away from my home to Gainesville, GA for Bible college. One of the toughest obstacles I had to face was finding housing. Everything was either way too expensive or not available. By the time I had to move, my only choice was to live with my great uncle who lived an hour away from the church and school.

Know this, that the discomfort of a season doesn't void the promise of the calling. God rarely calls us into comfort where everything is easy, beautiful, and just the best. His call is typically all about pushing through and bearing the uncomfortable moments during the journey so that He can tear up any false foundations that may have been laid. If you are serious about God's call then you will find that nothing could ever outweigh the desire to fulfil it. I was called and had to learn to give my all.

That early season was different for me. I lived in a basement. I was related to the people I lived with, but I didn't know them personally. I was shy and awkward, and stayed in my room most of the time. I didn't say or do much. I used to sneak around to see if they were gone, so I could do my laundry. Yeah, I was weird but that is just a small part of the personal discomfort I faced.

The discomfort of a season doesn't void the promise of the calling.

@caseyhodges
#walkingwithacompass

The Secret Place

While living there, I was trying to figure out what God had called me to specifically. I had stepped out and followed His voice but now I needed to put my hand to a plow and work. On top of everything, I was also dealing with sin that needed to be removed from my life (so that wasn't too encouraging). I soon labeled this my isolation season; like Moses finding God in the wilderness, I found Him in mine. It was lonely and hard, and I did not understand.

While I was busy trying to find another place to live, God was doing something I was not aware of - God allowed me to discover the treasures of my current surroundings. I had a whole basement to myself, quiet and empty, with nothing to distract me or hold me back from receiving what God was speaking to me. God began to reveal so much for me to grow in, for me to learn more about myself, and about Him.

Pressing into this season taught me the importance of having a dedicated devotional time. Private devotional time created a hunger and thirst in me for seeking God and establishing my relationship with Him. God showed me the secrets of the secret place. Once I had tasted and seen - I hungered for it. And He was always faithful to feed me from His hands.

Those months of isolation were one of the biggest blessings during the early moments of my calling. I look back at those moments I spent in prayer, reading 20-30 chapters of the Bible; and I

Sometimes it takes feeling like there is no one with you in order to find the One who is always with you.

@caseyhodges
#walkingwithacompass

know now that God was isolating me to mold me into what I needed to be for His work. I was all alone, but sometimes it takes feeling like there is no one with you in order to find the One who is always with you; the One who sticks closer than a brother.

Trusting God One Step at a Time

Even in the darkest nights when I felt unworthy, lost, and unqualified to be in the ministry, He was there. I would sit there and question what I was supposed to do next or what my calling looked like, but when I said, "yes," I was responding only to His voice. I was not responding to a full description of what my life would be like. I said "yes" to the King rather than what my future position or accomplishments might be.

I'm still very young in this calling, but I'm reminded daily of where I was and even where I am now. A constant pursuit of God will always have you changing and will help you recognize the lies that try to grip your heart. I had to learn that the thoughts that are against the will of God for my life are lies from the enemy. Because of these lies, I could have easily despised the small beginnings God led me to and moved on to try to make something of myself without God's help. This is what I like to call an Ishmael calling - a pursuit out of your fleshly desires. It fails every time, leaving us empty.

We wouldn't need much faith if God gave us a full rundown of our lives and everything that we would do. He called and I said "yes," even when I didn't know what it looked like. He was developing in me the compass that would guide me in my calling. The more practice you have in using the compass God gave you through the Holy Spirit, the easier it becomes to find your way and get to where God is calling you. Otherwise, trust me, the desires of your heart, when not pruned by God, will derail you in this walk every time. He wants to know if you are willing, without knowing direction. He wanted to see if I would be obedient to His voice, without seeing the final product of His work.

One thing to do when you are stepping out: Find yourself a God-fearing leader in your profession and see how their lives have played out (Heb. 13:7). For one, I believe that learning from what people have gone through pushes us with confidence if we face it as well. However, the most important thing to do is notice the working hand of the Lord.

He is faithful to fulfill every promise. If you look, you will gain trust and confidence in the beginning stages. Why? Because, when you see the progress of His work, you see the faithfulness of His promises. I am sure that when Jesus worked as a carpenter, customers trusted in His craft because they had seen the finished work of His hands, and along this journey you will too.

CHAPTER 3

PROTECTION

I have given you authority to trample on snakes and scorpions and to overcome the power of the enemy; nothing will harm you.

Luke 10:19 NIV

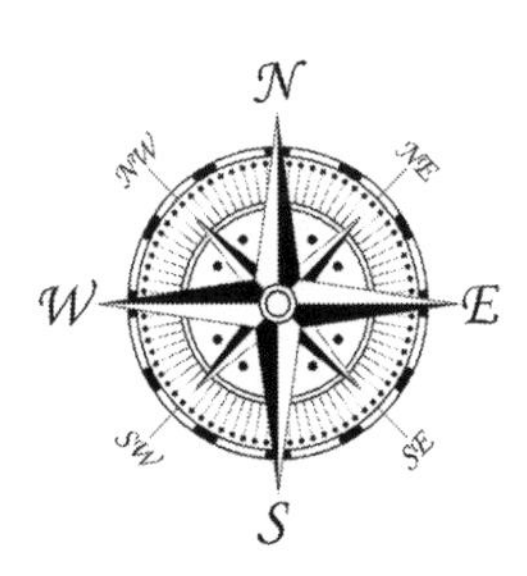

CHAPTER 3

PROTECTION

I can remember going camping when I was young and the experience of being surrounded by nature. It was a young boy's playground. I can remember the smell of the woods, the excitement of building a fire at night, and the sugar rush from all the roasted marshmallows. Honestly, at that age, I was just excited to sleep in a tent. That was one of the best parts of the whole trip. Call me crazy, but it was better than a hotel room! The smell of the air mattress, the sound of the bugs outside, and we even had a toilet! Well, a portable one anyways. We were high-class camping for sure, and I can remember my dad making a comment about it all being paid off (whatever that meant in a mind of a young kid)!

As you can tell I love camping. One of my dreams in life is to hike out and camp under the stars while watching the northern lights or to go on a camp and hunting trip. Just imagine waking up in the icy breeze of the morning and making a pot of coffee over a fire you built with your own hands - just like Bear Grylls, without all the eating bugs and stuff!

What I remember the most about our camping trips was a trail called *Snake Trail*. It was a dirt trail, with a few wooden bridges to cross along the way. It was a pretty straightforward path, but the excitement came from the name of it. We would walk it every time we went camping. The coolest thing about this trail was how many snakes you would see. I know the name should be a dead giveaway, but they were *everywhere*! Imagine hiking on a trail with no real sense of direction, knowing you could walk up on a snake at any moment. Of course, little Casey was just as confident as could be looking for a snake to bruise my heel. (Ha! Bible joke!)

A Heavenly Perspective

A lot of time, that is how we feel in life. We start this walk towards spiritual maturity. We pursue the call that God has placed on our lives. For the most part everything is going great; however, just like *Snake Trail*, these little snakes stay hidden just waiting for the right moment to strike at your feet. In the Bible, snakes represent the works of the enemy. The enemy will try his best to disguise himself along the trail to get you to look past the evil tactics of his plans. He will hide along your journey just like a snake and wait for the perfect moment to strike.

Do not fear! When you are using the compass of the Holy Spirit to guide your life, you will begin to see what others cannot. You will have a heavenly perspective to see what others do not. This will protect you from the lies, tactics, and deceptive plans of the wicked and prepare you for what may come.

We all know the saying, "good things come to those who wait." I'd add to that, "good things come to those who trust in the Lord and yield to His direction." When we position ourselves to yield and are willing to listen, we will receive the insight to see the things of the Lord. When we have that, nothing is hidden, and nothing is harmful. Even with hardships and challenges, through the lens of a heavenly perspective, you will believe that all things will work together for good.

Walking in Authority

In Luke chapter 10, we read that we will be given the authority to trample on the enemy and to overcome all of the enemy's power. While I wouldn't want to encourage you to purposely step on a snake (like little Casey wanted to), we have been given full authority through Christ to trample all over the enemy.

Just like a snake, the devil is ready to strike and inject his poison into your life. That poison can look like

Good things come to those who trust in the Lord and yield to His direction.

@caseyhodges

#walkingwithacompass

doubts, fears, lies, or shame. Though, when you walk in the authority of Jesus Christ, no matter when the enemy shows up and tries his best to get you, all you have to do is stand firm in the authority you have been given. You have all authority over the enemy through Jesus Christ, and you will overcome every weapon he throws your way.

"'No weapon formed against you shall prosper and every tongue which rises against you in judgment you shall condemn. This is the heritage of the servants of the Lord and their righteousness is from Me,' Says the Lord."
Isaiah 54:17 NKJV

I love the power that this verse can bring to any situation. However, let us not have this false expectation that we will never experience pain or hurt in life. Along the journey, we will face attacks, difficulties, and just plain sucky moments. God never promised an easy life without any troubles, but the truth and promise is that "it will not prosper." He promises us strength, protection, and love.

When we trust in the compass that God has given us through the Holy Spirit by praying, reading God's word, and spending time in His presence; we are safe in His love and protection. No matter the storm or attack, it will not overtake you and the battle will be yours. God will be there. We have a compass in

The compass of God calls you to do many things in private before it is announced publicly.

@caseyhodges

#walkingwithacompass

our hearts to lead us where we need to go even when the battle is raging.

Overcoming Doubt & Fear

Even Moses had to face moments of learning the power of God's compass. Just like us, he dealt with the doubt and fear of God's call on his life. In the seasons of my life when things were not clear, and I could not see how or what direction I was going in, I allowed cracks to form on the face of my compass. I could no longer see the direction of the needle. I thought my voice was too southern to preach. I thought that people would not understand me. (Yes, that was a real thought in my head).

Most days, following our calling will seem like a journey that's full of doubt on an uncharted path. It is easy to start hiking on a trail that has already been cleared ,but the ones who take the path less traveled with faith are the ones who make a real difference.

Moses, filled with doubt, had a moment with God. Time and time again, he was given direction. Moses was seeing the compass for the first time. God came to him in chapter 4 of Exodus and listed instructions for him to follow. It's crazy to me that God asked Moses to act out the signs and wonders before He put him in front of anyone else to perform them.

Sometimes God does it that way. He tells us our instructions privately, and we begin to do them internally before we express them outwardly. Sometimes the compass of God calls you to do many things in private before it is announced publicly. God gives us a compass and allows us to see and search for the things of God and His plans for us. Just like Moses had his doubts, we can have doubts too. And these doubts, if we do nothing about them, can alter the direction of our journey. Keep your compass protected and allow God to lead you in the way you need to go.

Peace in His Direction

I remember the new journey that I was on. I was trying to allow God to be the leader and Lord of my life to direct me and lead me into His ways. Some days it felt like I had no direction, other days I felt like the Lord was beside me, leading me and guiding me. Those moments were sweet and filled me with much joy. It was like the first time when he spoke the promise over me. I can tell you the best feeling is when you know that God is leading you, even when it seems scary.

I'm sure for Moses, the compass seemed a little broken at times, but he trusted the guiding power of it. Let your trust be in God and allow him to protect you in your journey along the way. He will never let you miss it, but you have to keep Him close to your heart to hear and listen for His direction.

In Colossians, 3:15, His Word says, "Let the peace of Christ rule in your hearts, since as members of one body you were called to peace. And be thankful." Let the peace of God rule in your hearts. There is no attack too big for the peace of God to comfort you. He is with you through the storm. He is there in the middle of the sinking ship. His peace is there for you.

Take a moment to think back on some God moments in your life. Maybe a moment when you thought you wouldn't make it, but somehow you did. Maybe something looked so far away, but God established it in you. That is what He wants for you to know; that He has you in His hands and to know that He has endless possibilities for you.

Stay Focused on the Truth

Do not be discouraged when your plans are changed by God's divine plans for your life. Fight against those thoughts of doubt. Doubt in what you are doing is a killer to where you are going. These thoughts come against me all the time. You and I have to learn to replace those thoughts: Thoughts of "I'm not enough," get replaced with "God has called me and anointed me for such a time as this."

Take the word of God and find scriptures to combat the negative lies of the enemy. Do not let the lies go against the compass in your life, which is the Word of God. Learn to know in your heart that what

Doubt in what you are doing is a killer to where you are going.

@caseyhodges
#walkingwithacompass

God can do is far greater than what you can do by yourself. He sees the burdens in this world. He is the answer and He will use you to accomplish it. Navigating through the promise should always be partnered with this scripture:

"And whatever you do, whether in word or deed, do it all in the name of the Lord Jesus, giving thanks to God the Father through him."
Colossians 3:17 NIV

We should wake up every day with the mindset to go out and work for the Lord, not for ourselves. God has called us into His Holy calling and with that comes an eternal weight. What we do on this earth has weight for what happens in eternity. The true promise of living is that in everything we do, we do it for the Lord.

We do not have to be Moses and lead millions of people out of slavery. Do all you do for the Lord. His being pleased with you is and will ever be the greatest fulfillment in life. The beauty about it is, He will surely embrace you with that fulfillment. Face the call of God for your life with excitement, even though it might scare you. Chase after it and trust God.

CHAPTER 4

PROVISION & BLESSING

And my God shall supply all your need according to His riches in glory by Christ Jesus.

Philippians 4:19 NKJV

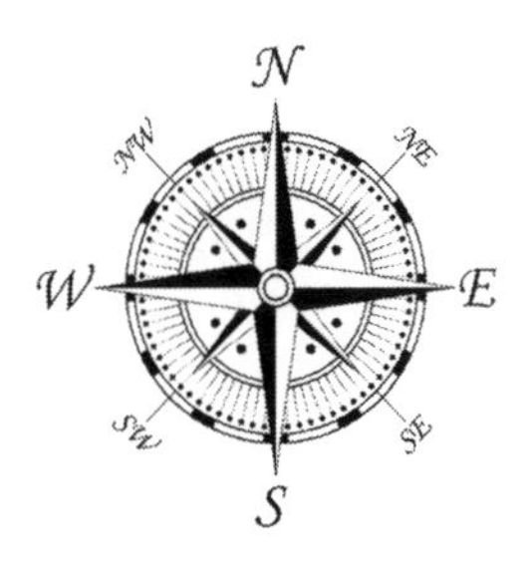

CHAPTER 4

PROVISION & BLESSING

It is impossible for the world to meet all of your needs. I have experienced a God that fulfills every need, but not every want. Let me say it like this: God doesn't always meet the want and the desire, but he will always meet the needs. He is the true provider, the true healer, and the true fulfillment of our souls. God is in the business of meeting our needs. He cares for and has the best interest of His children at heart.

I am reminded of King Solomon in the Bible when God asks him what he wants: God tells him He will give Solomon anything he wants: any riches, status, or materialistic thing! Solomon's heart was so in-tune with his calling that he knew what to ask for: He asked God for the wisdom he needed to lead the people.

God fulfills every need, but not necessarily every want.

@caseyhodges
#walkingwithacompass

What are the Desires of Your Heart?

You can tell real quick the root of one's heart by what they ask of God. Maybe we need to take inventory of our hearts and truly ask ourselves, "what is the desire within me?" "Am I seeking the will of the Father?" If so, "do I have the Father's interests in my heart"? If it is only for personal gain, my prayers would be for self-interest.

You have to see this as it is. Many people get mad because God didn't fulfill what they *wanted*. To fix this, we have to set our eyes on God and not this world. It is time to receive a heavenly perspective. God cares so much about you and His people. Just like King Solomon's prayer, it went beyond himself and in fact, touched a nation. Do our prayers go beyond just ourselves?

God provided every step of the way during this walk, and has fulfilled me in ways that I did not even know were possible. The compass that we have in this life is not to point us to self-success or materialistic riches but points us back to God and His will for us. If you read the Bible, you will find that God desires for His people to be successful and blessed. However, the difference is within the direction of the walk.

Are you following your self's desires? Or are you following the perfect will of God for your life? Trust me, the second option is filled with more blessings and favor then imaginable. The opposing forces will tell you otherwise, and they will try to distract you with something that *looks* fulfilling. You have to realize that the main goal in this life shouldn't be to reach some status or bank account number. The main goal is to draw close to God and live the life that God has given us: a life close to His heart and obedient to His words. Hold on to the life compass. He will direct and lead you into a life of everlasting, a life full of abundance, and God's provision.

Your Calling is a Threat to the Enemy

"But the more they were oppressed, the more they multiplied and spread; so the Egyptians came to dread the Israelites..."
Ex. 1:12 NIV

In the book of Exodus a new king arose. He felt threatened by the numbers of the children of Israel. The Scripture says that they multiplied more and spread abroad. Imagine being so fruitful that the enemy starts to worry about your increase. The Egyptians were afraid that the children of Israel might become too strong and overthrow them. The Bible says that the king gave orders to oppress the Israelites and make life difficult.

The king was a directional force; one that was trying to hold back the promises and favor of God's people. He wanted to oppress them because he was afraid. I don't know about you but I want to have favor that makes the enemy scared. God's promise for His people is to take them from Glory to Glory, and because of this, we must realize that people will look upon us and be envious. This doesn't give us the right to think of ourselves more than others, but to be humble in heart because of what God has done. When God provides the abundance, we must get ready to stand firm and endure towards the direction God has given us.

Take a moment and rejoice for what God is doing, because the enemy is afraid! Even if you may not see it now, go ahead and praise God for what will come. The enemy is afraid because your faith is multiplying! Your journey to spiritual maturity is growing.

The enemy doesn't want to be overthrown in your life. The enemy desires to have control over you and is seeking to do everything to stop you from reaching the true promise from God in your life. We may encounter people, jobs, and circumstances that seem as though they are trying to enslave us to the thoughts of the enemy over our lives. But rejoice for the victory on the journey is yours!

No one ever asked the people of Israel to overtake Egypt. The Egyptians just assumed they would out of fear. They lashed out towards God's people, and ended up enslaving the children of

Israel. You may relate to this in some way. You may be getting punished for something you didn't do, and it's only because someone assumed something about you.

This is what it looked like: the children of Israel were living free and loving life, and then the next day, they became the lowest of low. We may find ourselves in a similar position. One day you can be higher than the clouds, and then the next day, you may find yourself enslaved to your thoughts and the opinions of others. Scripture gives us clear instruction for this.

"Casting down arguments and every high thing that exalts itself against the knowledge of God, bringing every thought into captivity to the obedience of Christ."
2 Cor 10:5 NKJV

We have to learn to be strong at the beginning and receive the steadfast heart God gives us in Him. Understand that your provision from God may have a negative impact on the ones around you. Be careful of those who envy what you have and the vision given by God for your life. They will be nothing more than a scared king in your life trying to enslave you with faithless living and doubtful thinking.

God Gives You More than What You Put In

"And I will make the Egyptians favorably disposed toward these people so that when you leave you will not go empty-handed. Every woman is to ask her neighbor and any woman living in her house for articles of silver and gold and for clothing, which you will put on your sons and daughters. And so you will plunder the Egyptians."
Ex. 3:21-22 NKJV

This part of the story is one of my favorites. God told Moses to tell the people of Israel that they would leave Egypt with gold and fine clothing. They would be leaving Egypt blessed, coming out of slavery with more than they had. It is powerful to think that, as slaves, their only clothing was on their backs . I would guess, even what they had before entering slavery had been taken from them.

However, God showed great favor and mighty blessing in such a way that the children of Israel would ask for gold, silver, and clothing. God had blessed them in such a way that by the time they were leaving, it would have seemed as if they went and plundered everyone in Egypt, but they didn't take it; it was given to them.

God will bless you to an amount that it looks like you went and plundered, having more than you did before. You must listen when God calls you to something and begins to prepare you for where He is taking you. You will not go lacking. You will have plenty for the journey.

Blessing comes when faithfulness and obedience is shown in the call. God desires to bless you, dress you in favor, and give you good gifts. He is such a loving Father. Don't despise the beginning of your call or compare it to someone else's 10-year journey because they have more opportunity, connections, and trust with leaders than you. You don't know what beginning stages they went through to get where they are. God wants to develop you in the beginning; so that when these times come, you don't trade Him out for what He gave you.

When we face our Egypt, (those days of enslavement) we may feel overwhelmed by our fears, doubts, or even the unknown. But God showed up for me, and He will for you. He gave me His promise and He has one for you. He showed me the sweetness of His presence.

I look back on earlier days when I had no idea what I was doing, no sense of worth, was entangled in my flesh and it seemed like I had no hope for anything. However, I also remember the tears, the prayers, and the breakthrough. I remember what I left those days with: strength, hope, a future, and confidence.

When God took me to another season, I left the old one as if I had plundered it and taken everything

God meant for me to take. I left with the purest gold of worship, the silver of surrender, and the finest clothes of righteousness. I left with much more than what I came with.

God took me through that season. I can now see what He did and how He met my needs. Most of what I desire isn't what I needed to grow and mature. We can think that getting on a big stage or platform will grow and mature us to what God has in store for us. But does it? I believe that the stage and lights only grow the gifting but it's off the stage that grows the character to sustain the gift. I have realized that I would prefer learning in the environment of God's safety rather than in the audience of man. In the presence of God, there is a Father in the audience, cheering for you.

God's Promise Never Changes

The imparting of the Holy Spirit is the great provision that humans need. It is a freely given tool for life. It was God's gift for us, through his Son that brought us into a relationship with Him. Now through righteousness, God is here with us. We have more now, leaving what has enslaved us. Through Christ; He is leading us and guiding our every footstep. Even when we get it wrong, the promise is still there.

The children of Israel went through the wilderness over and over because of disobedience.

The stage and lights only grow the gifting but it's off the stage that grows the character to sustain the gift.

@caseyhodges
#walkingwithacompass

But the thing that never changed was the promise and God's hand over their lives. There is joy in knowing that even when we fail and mess up, the promises of God, the grace, and the mercy of God are still there for us. He loves you and will never give up on you. Even if you fail, you still have the compass to lead you into the promised land for your life. Protect that compass; it is what you received as a blessing to help in the navigation of life.

God told Moses everything that he needed to do. He provided every step and direction for the children of Israel. From that moment in Egypt, God stepped in. When they began the journey, God provided a cloud by day and a fire by night (foreshadowing of the Holy Spirit). It was the compass for the children of Israel. It led them in the way that they should go. God provided heavenly food that was delivered to them every morning. God kept up his part, like always.

He said in His Word that he will never leave nor forsake us (Heb. 13:5). Just like the children of Israel, God's promises will always stand the test of time. He provides every step. The step of obedience usually leads to drawing closer to Him and His Word. But He ends up leading you by way of His will.

Trust God and not the situation. Seek Him and not the "I can do it myself" mentality. Seek Him above all else and respond with obedience. Watch the Lord lead and guide you through life. He will always come through no matter what.

The biggest direction you can take in your life is completely trusting in God. Trusting in God will lead you into victory and an abundance of life. Hold that compass close to your heart, and do not let the enemy have any force against it.

Trust God and the process. He will bless, protect, and provide every step of the way. He will never see the righteous forsaken, and He will always make a way when there seems to be no way (Is. 43:19). I hope you will find trust and obedience towards God and watch the providing hand of a loving Father meet every need you have. Remember He loves you!

Trust God and the process.

@caseyhodges
#walkingwithacompass

CHAPTER 5

COUNTERFEIT

In which you once walked according to the course of this world, according to the prince of the power of the air, the spirit who now works in the sons od disobedience.

Ephesians 2:2 NKJV

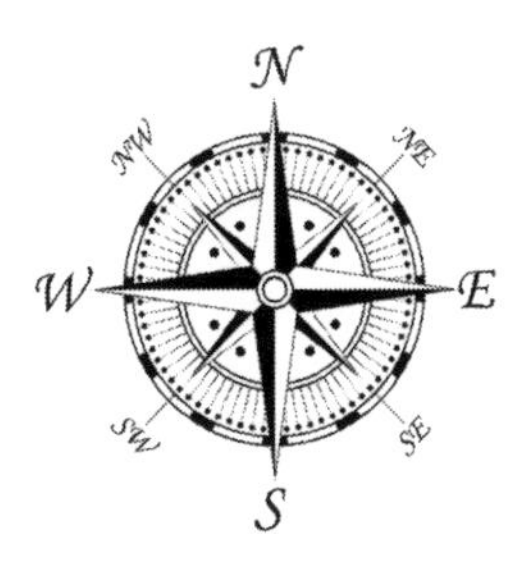

CHAPTER 5

COUNTERFEIT

Every time I read Ephesians 2:2, I see the importance of staying awake and aware of the enemy at work. In Ephesians, Paul tells us that the prince of the power of the air is at work. One of the enemy's tactics is to interrupt our path and open opportunities for disobedience. The nature of our made-up being is fallen and faulty. You and I can naturally lead ourselves on a path opposite to God's purpose. We have the choice between our desires in the flesh vs. God's loving design for our life in Him.

Recognizing Opposing Forces

The journey toward our callings and purpose in life will lead us on an amazing path. God has some mighty doors ready to open; great opportunities that we could not give to ourselves nor accomplish through the flesh. We must be aware - that although we have God on our side, we also have an enemy to fight alongside our flesh. We have an enemy whose purpose is to stop us from reaching and fulfilling the God-given potential in our lives. And the enemy's deceptions can be well-hidden in ministry work, living a false idea of a "godly life", and or a "doing your best" mentality. All this may be true and feel good, but it can also can be empty and ineffective compared to what God can do.

Discovering the promise comes with discovering that there is an opposing force. Many forces come against us each day to try and pull us in the opposite direction God has for us. We have the natural force within us of fallen nature. As a believer, you have the force of the Holy Spirit. However, we also contend with the forces of darkness.

A compass' needle direction is determined by the force of the Earth's magnetic field. As you walk through life, there are forces pulling on you from every direction. You may feel the force of a fallen world or even the force of the Holy Spirit. But without a doubt, there is always something coming against us or a force trying to push us towards the truth.

We know that when the enemy comes with force, it leaves us paralyzed and helpless without God. When God comes to us with His empowerment, we become more than conquerors and more than able to accomplish what we are made to do. We overcome the enemy's forces by the power of God, but the truth is, we as humans are susceptible to falling. We can all agree that most of time, the direction we walk is accompanied by our desires. You can bet if heading south leads me to a million dollars then I wouldn't waver on staying the path. But while I'm pursuing God, His desires are imparted into me and now I walk, not of my flesh, but of the Spirit.

The Battles Within Our Souls

Since the creation of Adam and Eve, we are descendants of a fallen nature. We need the redemption and love of God to come and save us from ourselves and the sin that so easily entangles us. We need Him to empower us with His Holy Spirit so we can stand against the forces that come to shift our direction away from God. These invisible fields that pull at our compass' direction are very powerful and it is important to be watchful of them.

We cannot control the compass by force of our own strength, the Scriptures say, "God is our refuge and strength, an ever-present help in trouble." (Psalm 46:1-3) Let the force within that scripture drive us to a powerful strength only found in Jesus Christ. Declare that right now and say it with confidence and assurance in Christ. "HE IS MY STRENGTH!" We must come against the wicked forces with the truth of God's word. If we hesitate to come into this knowledge, we can wander through life with the lies that we hold onto.

The biggest battle of our lives isn't of this world. The battle is within our souls, the very hearts that beat within our chests. Raging within us all is a constant battle between the very thing we were created to do and the nature of our flesh. The thoughts of confidence vs. the reality of the doubt we feel. The failure part of us that we know more than anyone else vs. the grace that God extended to help us to keep going. The battle within is fierce and does not let up. The goal for you and me is not to achieve temporary success but to have the internal acceptance of the Father burning strong within our hearts. This empowers us to reach further and to do greater than our ability in the flesh.

Don't Delay your Promises

In the book of Exodus, the children of Israel are a great example of how easily we can be affected by the different forces that come against us. The story shows the people of God were given a promise of a land flowing with milk and honey. God then delivered Israel out of bondage and captivity. On their journey, Israel set their focus and goal to reach the promise from God and follow Him with all their lives. The sad thing about their journey through the wilderness is the wasted time and how long they delayed their possession of the land.

We have a lot to learn from the children of Israel. If we are not careful, we are capable of delaying and wasting time reaching the promises. In God's Word,

He promises that what He speaks never returns void. His word will always come to pass. It wasn't God's fault the children of Israel didn't yield to His directional leading. It was an easy step to come out of bondage from Egypt but they fell right back into it with their own doubt, fear, and complaining.

The children of Israel would eventually find themselves walking through the wilderness of their own ways. This not only delayed them from the promise, it hindered them from receiving it in their hearts. God didn't throw away the promised land. He gave it to their descendants. God will eventually give your promise to someone else if you hinder the moment of receiving it. See the children of Israel received the freedom from Egypt but they were blinded by themselves, the situation, and the same mountain over and over again. They gave up on the fullness of the promise.

The Israelites said to them,

"If only we had died by the LORD's hand in Egypt! There we sat around pots of meat and ate all the food we wanted, but you have brought us out into this desert to starve this entire assembly to death."
Exodus 16:3 NIV

The children of Israel began to realize their position in the wilderness and not the design of the process. The position will always outweigh every process, development, and teaching that we need. Our flesh wants nothing but position because in the eyes of the flesh position looks good and comfortable.

The complaints of the children of Israel started to overtake the word of the Lord during their journey. The children of Israel wished to be back in Egypt (bondage). They desired to have what they did in Egypt.

Let's ask a humbling question: would we prefer to live with bondage to something and achieve the "false glory of the promise?" Or to live with freedom and be effective wherever the Lord leads? Know that freedom requires yielding of oneself and the discipline of constant obedience.

In the wilderness and promised land, the Lord is leading. The Israelites listed all they had in Egypt. The deception of the enemy will get you to remember what you had to distract you from what God is trying to do (just like Adam and Eve). You cannot obey God while trying to number and order your desires. I don't know about you, but I would rather be free in Christ, in the wilderness, than enslaved to the wickedness with the pleasures of this world.

Counterfeit Fulfillment

"The lions may grow weak and hungry, but those who seek the Lord lack no good thing."
Psalm 34:10 NIV

This scripture speaks so profoundly to this world and our walk through it. It becomes our nature to seek out and devour the things of our flesh. We desire and lust after whatever may spike our interest. Fleshly desires may be sexual lust, greed for money, success for status, or security within our insecurities. We all have that one thing that we seek to fulfill.

Rather than seeking the direction of God, we seek the interests of our flesh. You may be working a 9 to 5 job to get by, instead of living out the God-given purpose for their life. Have faith, step out, and follow the direction of the compass given to you by God.

We are meant to live a whole and fulfilled life. God made us to long for companionship. As humans, we get our fulfillment from relationships and intimacy. The forces of this world do a great job bringing us counterfeit fulfillment. We often trade what God offers us for a temporary fix or a "one-night stand." Most of us are looking for something to give us that sense of high and excitement for living life. God is offering knowledge and a relationship to all who seek Him. A relationship beyond this life and knowledge beyond our understanding.

We put so much emphasis on relationships and intimacy with humans. We create other distractions that can steal us away and provide counterfeit fulfillment. God convicted me recently. It was silly, to be honest, but it was the truth.

I started playing *Call of Duty* with a great friend of mine. It was our time to get our minds off other stuff and have fun; however, an interest in video games started to take over. Hobbies are not bad and having fun is not bad. We all need an activity to rest and refresh ourselves. But I found myself thinking more about the game than I did about my calling or even my intimacy with God, and it became a counterfeit compass.

God pricked my heart as I waited for the game to download and add all its new updates. As I sat there waiting for the next 30-45 minutes, He said, "You would sit here and wait on this, but would rush our time together and not wait with me." I was like "whaaat??" I immediately turned it off and went and checked myself in my spirit.

Lesson learned: take heed to the correction and the still small voice that calls you closer to the life-giving relationship He made available for us.

Don't Look Back

"For whatever was written in former days was written for our instruction, that through endurance and through the encouragement of the Scriptures we might have hope."
Romans 15:4 NKJV

I believe if we learn from our failures and from the examples of others who walk in this faith, we will better ourselves to see and know the help of the Holy Spirit. The compass, or Holy Spirit, is a tool to bring you closer to God. It provides a way to grow and mature you into who He has called you to be. It will direct you through life's journeys and anything that may come with them. The compass doesn't lead us around battles, but will give us what we need to continually walk in victory through any battle.

Another battle is glorifying what you used to have and discounting what God may be doing in your life presently. I still have days when the enemy wants to attack with this tactic. It's so easy to look back or take a look at your life now and say "I could be here by now," or "I could have this and that, life would be great." The enemy will begin to highlight in your mind what you used to have or what you could have. You must know that when the enemy comes against you, it will always go against God and His will for your life.

The compass doesnt' lead us around battles, but will give us what we need to continually walk in victory through any battle.

@caseyhodges
#walkingwithacompass

The enemy does not care about your success, money, or relationships. He only cares about the weakness or vulnerability in you for those things. He wants you to compromise your character rather than develop it for God. His main goal is to stop you from reaching your full potential in Christ. If he can hinder your growth in Christ, he is on the right track to accomplishing his goal - and that is to steal, kill, and destroy.

Let me point out one thing. If you are questioning whether or not you need a particular hobby, relationship, or job; it will not fulfill you nor give you what you truly need. God is the only path of fulfillment in our lives. He is the peace that you need. Knowing that He accepts us and calls us into His family is the assurance we need to fight the enemy's lies. Hold on to the compass and let the Word of God direct you through this life. Let the Word of God give you the confidence and assurance you need to be fulfilled and equipped for your calling. Stand strong against the false compass and the lies of it. Do not let it derail you from where God is taking you!

CHAPTER 6

HIS NAME

Therefore, God also has highly exalted Him and given Him the name which is above every name.

Philemon 2:9 NKJV

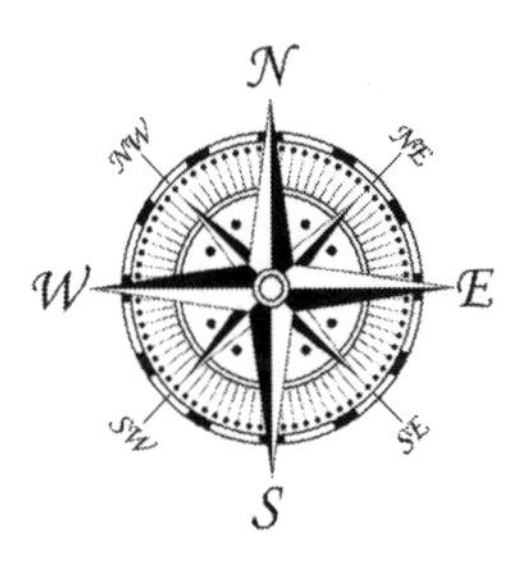

CHAPTER 6

HIS NAME

Let us take a moment to say the name of Jesus. Say it over and over if you need to. I have learned that each utterance of His name opens a door for God to answer you in any situation. Have you ever had God answer you? I can say that I am not yet to a place where He answers in the form of a burning bush or an audible voice.

A Call to Write

For example, the answer and direction for this book came from God speaking through someone else. My wife and I were listening to a podcast about the topic of worship. I turned it on because I thought my wife needed it. I thought to myself, "well, maybe she can learn something in this." As it happened, I was wrong for not expecting God to speak to me as well, but he got my attention anyway.

There was a part of the podcast that said, "Some of y'all have settled with writing blogs, instead of the book God told you to write." When I heard that, it was like a piercing heart moment. I knew it was for me to hear because I had the leading from God to write a book. The thing that stopped me was self-doubt, worry, and even the thought: "It will not be good enough to make money." All the wrong reasons - I know.

At that moment, I was like "geeezz, God. I mean, in front of my wife, too. You had to expose me like that." But He was right. I always had the ambition to write a book. I struggled with the particular thought to write, and it was an insecurity for me. I never was good at writing. As a child I hated taking spelling tests at school or writing stories for class. I taught myself to believe that I was not good at it.

My view has changed. I may not be the best, but God spoke and is faithful. Even if I have to go through more edits then most writers; I will trust more in who called me to the task. I rely on Him to use the same kid that could not spell in school to write a book and reach people for His name.

So when I heard that podcast, I knew right then that God brought up the task again of writing a book. I have tried a few times before to start writing, but I would always stop because I listened to the lies instead of His voice that called me. I realize that God has graced me to do this, and even when I think, "it isn't good," He is still good.

The Name of God

I love the scripture Acts 1:8 "But you will receive power when the Holy Spirit has come upon you, and you will be my witnesses in Jerusalem and in all Judea and Samaria, and to the end of the earth."

God is calling you as a witness to His name, not a status for your name. Let Him work in your life and deal rightfully with you. You will become the image that He desires, the image of Him. Take the first step in obedience but be intentional with the next step.

He is our Comforter - His name and His still small voice embraces us like a loving father. As we seek His will and relationship, we begin to understand the direction. Many of us may struggle financially, concerned about money for our next meal or rent payment. But when we hear the name, Jehovah Jireh, all peace comes, and a directional mind-shift happens. Know He is the true provider, and if He has called you, He will sustain you.

Maybe you are facing sickness and see no hope. Your family member that you love is hurting, weak, and sick. You plead to God time and time again but nothing. You may get mad and think all hope is lost. But once you begin to speak the name, Jehovah Rapha, everything changes. God is the true Healer. God is the One that can take away all sickness and pain.

God is calling you as a witness to His name, not a status for your name.

@caseyhodges
#walkingwithacompass

We must realize that God's name is the direction we need within our hearts. I love knowing that whatever struggle, hardship, or temptations we face, He has a name to combat those very things. It is a shift in direction when I am struggling, but I know the Prince of Peace. Maybe it doesn't look like I have enough, but He is more than enough. This life may throw whatever it can but know that the sure foundation for your soul is Christ Jesus. And He is more than enough.

We are bombarded with names every day. And if you are like me, you might not be good with remembering the names of others. Please understand, this goes beyond a physical name. What are you labeling in your life? Are you calling yourself stupid? Are you saying you are worthless? What negative names do you speak that paralyzes you from the true direction of God? His name and the names that He carries are the hope and truth we need. It will brighten the darkest days. You will have strength when things are tough.

His name is the compass we need. I love the name, Yahweh. We sing praises about Yahweh and call on God with the same name He revealed to Moses.

"God said to Moses, "I AM WHO I AM.
This is what you are to say to the Israelites:
'I AM has sent me to you.'"
Exodus 3:14 NKJV

In this story, Moses asks God what shall I say to them of the one who sent me, and God answers back and says, "I AM." or "Yahweh." The name Yahweh is connected to breathing. Through the years the letters, A and E, were added into Yahweh. Originally it was spelled YHWH, mimicking the sound of a breath. God's name is the breath we breathe daily! Every moment of every day, as we take breaths - we breathe the name of God. Take note that today alone, you have probably spoken the name of God more times than you can count. His name is the compass we need and the breath we breathe.

His name is the compass we need and the breath we breathe.

@caseyhodges
#walkingwithacompass

CHAPTER 7

YOUR DESTINATION

I will guide you along the best pahtway for your life. I will advise you and watch over you.

Psalm 32:8 NLT

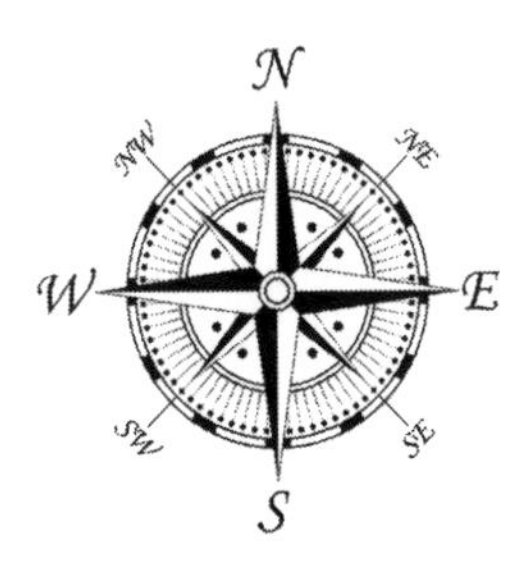

CHAPTER 7

YOUR DESTINATION

Throughout the Bible, God takes people through difficult situations and circumstances. It is almost like a pattern. God works through a difficult situation to bring us to a oneness with Him to fulfill His purpose and plan.

I can say with some certainty that with any calling comes some difficulties. Facing hardship will bring you closer to the heart of God and His plans for your life. Usually, when God allows certain things to happen, he wants to bring us closer to Him so we will rely and depend on Him more than we do ourselves or the promise He has given us. If God never brings us into alignment with His plan we would try to make things happen in our own ways. We cannot accomplish all God has for us in our own way or by depending on our own strength about God Himself.

Inward Direction

The children of Israel had their direction to the promised land. It never changed. It was there, God said it, and it was so. But what changed after that was the working within the heart. The Israelites complained and looked for an answer from God. God was not there to fix the outward but the inward. He gave them the direction needed to go to the promised land. Their complaining hearts derailed their trust in God which led to a change in direction from receiving the promised land.

I learned when God speaks - it can come as an outward change of direction, but it could also be an inward change of sanctification in the heart. We want the physical direction over the internal, that is why we are always looking for God to speak a new direction over our lives. We think it may be a new place, a new job, or a new opportunity. Allowing this to cloud our thoughts and motives hinders what God actually may be trying to do.

We may miss the change of direction within the heart that He is speaking to. This change is the one that matters. It's the change that prepares us for the destination of God. We cannot think that God will call us and then leave us. He walks beside us daily. And know this, having a call on your life doesn't mean you are perfect or that hardships are eliminated. The beauty about our God is He will call you. He will also change you and be with you through it all.

The Next Best Thing

Many times during this journey, I could have gone in another direction. That other direction would have been my second best - thinking I could take this in my own hands and do more. I like to call it a temporary fix, like the experience of wearing a new shirt. You get a new shirt and love how it looks and feels. Soon, after some time, it is just another shirt in your closet. Similarly, we can adapt this same pattern into our lives and find ourselves feeling unfulfilled in our new season or new dream - the same dream that we may have been so excited for before.

We navigate through life with these so-called mile markers. We reach a stage in life and search for what best fits a sense of satisfaction. For instance, try and recall your childhood and teenage years. Maybe like me, you would stare at TV commercials and search for the next, best toy. Years later, you are sixteen and desire that cool, new car to drive. We grow up in life, hoping a relationship will bring us some level of satisfaction. Even in the later stages of life, some are still searching for that next thing.

A Willingness to Sacrifice it All

In Genesis, chapter 22, God tells Abraham to sacrifice his son. God says, "Go and take your son to the land of Moriah, and offer him there as a burnt offering on a mountain which I will show you." God calls Abraham to do a task without giving him the whereabouts.

Our calling is similar to this story. God will call us and not tell us the full extent of the calling. We receive just enough direction to see if we are willing to obey. You must understand that this direction is not an unfair or discouraging circumstance. God does this to find who is willing to give it all up for Him - the ones who are obedient even to the point of sacrificing everything.

To fulfill the purpose of the kingdom in your life, God may call you to give up your time, money, job, or dream. Many people give in but later give up. They do not like uncertainty, nor do they like giving away control of their lives. We live in a day where controlling every aspect of our lives is normal.

Imagine what Abraham would have missed out on if he did not go or if he was not willing to sacrifice his son. God saw and stopped him at that moment because He saw the willingness of Abraham's heart to obey. The heart must be tested and found pleasing to God. He will then open up a mighty door and grant you something beyond your reach. For Abraham, that was the father of the nations.

We can see more examples of these "mile-markers" in other biblical characters when we look at the faith chapter in Hebrews (Hebrews 11). Take a moment and read through this chapter. Hopefully you did it, because the chapter itself has a topic that can propel you through each milestone, directional change, and inward obedience. This is the kind of faith that is required to trust God enough that you are willing to take a simple step of obedience that ultimately leads you down the path of your purpose.

Imagine giving up your son to unlock a God-given blessing in your life. A blessing that allows you to have a generational impact instead of a "just for the moment" impact. Research the stories and lives of well-known pastors or servants of God. They did not get the legacy by giving up only half of their lives or going through the motions of doing good and loving the Lord. The life we are willing to give up unlocks the supernatural life we will partake. The moment of willingness and obedience are together unlocking the undiscoverable favor and anointing of God in our lives.

Your Measure of Grace

I look up to a few faith fighters in my life to know that God is still working and moving faithfully. T.F. Tenny is one of my all-time favorites in the faith. I recall watching his old messages and his ability to deliver the Word of God with passion and conviction. I can remember the first and only time I heard him preach live. He was on his way to be with the Lord, most didn't know, but he was closer to eternity than most thought. He could barely walk, but when he got behind the pulpit to preach, he was a different man. He didn't just do it to do it. He gave the message everything he

The life we are willing to give up unlocks the supernatural life we will partake.

@caseyhodges
#walkingwithacompass

had, and it was amazing to see the measure of grace working through his gifting, but even more so, the anointing and dependency he still had even at that stage of life.

We rely on our *measure of grace*. What do I mean? Well, as the Word of God says, "all have been given a measure of grace." (Rom. 12:3) This grace is our gifts, talents, and strengths. We learn what those are as we progress in life, but most people do not live in that measure.

I have come to realize our measure is great for a kickstart into God's supernatural. I also have to be willing to lay my measure down to revive His supernatural blessings in my life. We hold onto the measure because it's a natural ability. We begin to live in the supernatural when we lay down our gifts. At that moment, we put our confidence in God and what He can accomplish through us.

God Directs Your Steps

I started out working in youth ministry for a short time. I chose that field of ministry because it felt like the only opportunity for a young minister, such as myself. I stuck with it for a while and learned. I grew in areas that I needed to, but youth ministry was not my calling. I had to accept this truth even though it seemed like most big-name pastors started in youth ministry. I soon learned not to attempt to replicate someone's call and walk with God. It will leave you empty because you will never know what it was that God had planned for you, what God called YOU to.

So, I was at a stop sign with a question mark on it. "What is there for me to do, God? What is my calling? Is there a particular area in the ministry that you are calling me?" I had no idea what to do.

God started to move after dedicated prayer, fasting, and wise counsel. I did not realize at the time how important the role of a mentor is in your life. I met Pastor Robert Stella. It was an out of the blue kind of connection. It started with a simple invite. I was unaware of the future influence and impact that a simple conversation in his office started in my life.

I was willing enough to sit down with a stranger. I was uncomfortable for a moment as I tried to make conversation, but now I lead and work under his guidance. The opportunity to call him my mentor and leader was a door God unlocked for me. God said "He will lead us and protect us" (Ps. 32:8) and "He will direct our steps" (Prov. 16:9). In that season of my life, I saw first-hand what God meant. I didn't know what God was doing; but, when I was unsure, God was confident.

Hold on to the compass. You will have the assurance that God is leading and directing your steps. There will be times when you don't know where to go or what to do. There is a compass within your grasp. It is the tool allowing us to walk out of this life and into the fullness and the abundance that God calls us to. What He requires from us is the same that He wanted to see in Abraham - the obedience, willingness, and readiness to give it all up for Him. Is it easy? No! But, one man's act of obedience unlocked a path for generations of others to reap from its benefits.

The Importance of Relationship

While writing this book, one of my best friends welcomed a baby boy, Gideon, into their lives. It leads me to think about the final topic: the power of a new life. The amazing thing about Gideon is he will soon discover what he likes and dislikes. He will have to go through life in all its seasons and see the wonders of the world. But like all of us, he will come to a point where he finds Jesus for himself - a true relationship with many tears and joys.

You may be reading this and still don't know for yourself who God is. Maybe you've heard about him from friends or family. You may have come across a Christian post on social media that you thought it sounded good at the time. The truth is, none of this will give you the true fulfillment that comes from a relationship with Him.

I know for myself, growing up and learning about God was difficult. We can hear so many do's and don'ts in learning and following God. Over time, this may harden our hearts and make it even more difficult to receive Christ into our lives. We must learn Christianity is not about changing someone because they are in sin or their life is not the image of God. We need to get back to the love and acceptance of Jesus

Christ. If we do not have this, we will spend more time hindering people than showing them the trueness of God.

It is not man who leads others to repentance; so what makes us think we are the ones who accept and change someone from sinner to believer? An intimate relationship with God changes the heart of us all. We cannot do it for ourselves, and we definitely cannot for someone else. The Bible clearly states, "only the love of God draws men/women to repentance" (Rom. 2:4 NKJV). Notice that it said "only the love." It does not mention our ability, possessions, or position. No, it says by the love of God, and that only comes from a relationship.

The Love of Christ

One of the greatest moments in my life was marrying my wife. She's my best friend and life partner. Our relationship together is filled with moments of learning and growing. Welcome to marriage - right?! We try hard not to focus on faults; but instead, move to loving and listening.

My wife could never change me by constantly picking at my faults. I would eventually turn away. My shortcomings would remain hidden, rather than received with love. Fortunately, she chooses to listen and shows love to me. We then discuss and out of the trust in the relationship between us we help each other grow and mature. As a result, she will always have a voice in my life to help me become a better me.

Our relationship with Christ is the same. No one wants to follow and be in a relationship with someone that constantly tells us what we are doing wrong. We must know that the love that He has for each of us and the power of His love changes us for the better. We do not change due to His wrath to smite us. The earth does not have to swallow us up like in Old Testament stories. He removes all guilt or shame and leads us into his glory for all eternity. God chooses to do this by His love.

Our goal in life should not be to become the next big thing or wealthiest person in the world. Our goal should be to show the love of Christ. We should be willing to give our lives for His purpose daily. If success and money come, then great. I still believe God loves to bless His children. We need to have that position of a child towards Him. We are adopted and loved by Him. A lifestyle that says no matter what I have or don't have - my God is enough for me. For He is a good Father.

You Have Arrived

God is at the center of our hearts. We have a compass, a tool, that is given by him to teach and to show us the way of life. This compass comes in three ways: Relationship with God, Obedience towards God, and the Work of the Holy Spirit.

No matter what I have or don't have - my God is enough for me.

@caseyhodges

#walkingwithacompass

We are led by the works of his hand and the power of His spirit. We need reverent fear, obedience, and more of His Holy Spirit in our lives. The Bible says, "But when he, the Spirit of truth, comes, he will guide you into all the truth. He will not speak on his own; he will speak only what he hears, and he will tell you what is yet to come." (Jn. 16:13) Open your heart and allow God to show you the gifts of life. You have the power inside of you to change the environment around you for His glory and honor.

This compass that you have is to lead you through life. Not without hard times or great riches and success; but instead, to the fullness of God's plan (and what comes from it; count it as a blessing). The beauty is when we align ourselves with God, we receive more than this world can offer.

This world has a compass of temporary benefits and self-pleasure. The world can only benefit you in the here and now. People will move across cities to try to get the promotion with the pay increase, the bigger house, and the American Dream life. In turn, they give up the church that loves them for who they are. They give up their relationship with Christ for the materials of this world. When we settle for the quick and easy life, the compass goes blurry. We end up lost and unfulfilled at the end of life.

God offers a compass of salvation, righteousness, and possibilities. I love the story of the respected Pastor, Pastor Jentezen Franklin. God called him to pastor a small church located in Gainesville, GA.

It may have been hard, but the compass within his heart led him there. It led him to God's possibilities within the church of Free Chapel and the city of Gainesville, GA. This small church now has campuses on the West Coast and East Coast. Supernatural growth can happen when you listen and obey the compass of the Holy Spirit within your heart, unleashing God's possibilities.

We need to stay strong and fight the good fight of faith. The compass within your heart is leading and guiding you through life. Be careful of what compass you follow. The Bible tells us those who walk in the flesh, reap the flesh. Those who walk in the Spirit will reap life, and that leads us to an eternity in Heaven with God. (Gal. 6:8)

That is the destination of the compass of God - to have the end of your life looking more like Christ and accomplishing all He has set out for you to fulfill. Let us live life to its fullness in God on this earth and eagerly wait to spend all of eternity in Heaven with Him. God has you right where he wants you. Be sensitive and allow the compass of God to lead you along life's journeys.

Every day I wake up with this compass as my tool. I go after what God has called me to do. The Holy Spirit will remain to help, guide, and lead me in the way of Christ. I need to remain sensitive and obedient to the leading of the compass.

God has called you - you need only to listen and obey. I knew He called me to write this book, but

I had to understand He was not writing it for me. I had to step out and do it. It has been a step-by-step walk - not a hop and a skip. When you step out, know that it isn't a walk where you will have all the knowledge of every step, but rather a trust and dependency on Christ establishing your steps along the way. If you live by the leading of the Holy Spirit, then you allow yourself to trust in the Lord. You will not lean on your understanding.

I would not be in a position to pursue my calling by leaning on my own understanding. I had to use the tool God had given me to live through life. That tool is the compass of the Holy Spirit.

As you go on through life - lean on that leading. Trust that God is walking with you, holding you by the hand. His gift to us is the Holy Spirit, and it is ever-present in your life, it is your tool! Take hold of that and use it to its full potential. You can do it! God is with you, and you have the greatest tool ever given to you. That is the compass of the Holy Spirit!

"I press on toward the goal to win the prize for which God has called me heavenward in Christ Jesus."
Philemon 3:14 NKJV

@caseyhodges
#walkingwithacompass

Made in the USA
Columbia, SC
27 October 2023

25089904R00061